From Tee To Green

From Tee To Green

A Book of Uncommon Prayers for Golfers

Text by Michael G. Lawler
Photographs by Brian Morgan

TWENTY-THIRD PUBLICATIONS
Mystic, Connecticut

For Michael

Twenty-Third Publications
P.O. Box 180
Mystic, CT 06355
(203) 536-2611

All photographs are by Brian Morgan: Golf Photography International (9 Carrick St., Glasgow, Scotland). Used with permission.

Cover designed by William Baker
Book edited and designed by John G. van Bemmel

ISBN 0-89622-323-x

Contents

Introduction   *vii*

1   *A Prayer at a Journey's Beginning*   *1*
Photo: Cherry Hills, Colorado

2   *A Prayer of Thanks and Praise*   *3*
Photo: Elk River, South Carolina

3   *A Prayer for Wisdom*   *5*
Photo: Doral, Florida

4   *A Prayer for Courage*   *7*
Photo: Inverness, Ohio

5   *A Prayer to Tread the Narrow Way*   *9*
Photo: Britannia, Grand Cayman, Bahamas

6   *A Prayer to Love Samaritans*   *11*
Photo: Honors Course, Tennessee

7   *A Prayer for Light*   *13*
Photo: Mountain Shadow, Arizona

8   *A Prayer for Humility*   *15*
Photo: Casa de Campo, Dominican Republic

9   *A Prayer for Refreshment*   *17*
Photo: Plainfield, New Jersey

10   *A Prayer for Renewal*   *19*
Photo: Oakland Hills, Michigan

11 *A Prayer in Selective Praise of Creation* 21
Photo: Bonita Bay, Florida

12 *A Prayer of Thanks for Revelation* 23
Photo: Eagle Trace, Florida

13 *A Prayer for Golfers*
Photo: Bear Creek, California

14 *A Prayer for Perseverance* 27
Photo: Desert Highlands, Arizona

15 *A Prayer for Life* 29
Photo: Shoal Creek, Alabama

16 *A Prayer for Fruitfulness* 31
Photo: Colonial, Texas

17 *A Prayer for Forgiveness* 33
Photo: Sawgrass, Florida

18 *A Prayer at a Journey's End* 35
Photo: Wild Dunes, South Carolina

19 *A Prayer for Election* 37
Photo: Castle Pines, Colorado

Introduction

I first played golf when I was ten. I caught a bug then against which I still have no immunity. For the past forty-three years I have golfed my way across four continents (some day I will play in Australia), alternately marveling and cursing at golf courses. For most of that time I looked on them as the creations of architects with such recognizable names as old Tom Morris, young Tom Morris, Pete Dye, Jack Nicklaus. It has been only in recent years that I have come to realize that they are also the creations of the Creator-God.

When I was younger, I thought of creation as something that God did way back then in the beginning, in some exotic Eden-Garden. That view reflected a certain model of both creation and the God who effected it. Creation had been achieved and the Creator was now at rest on an eternal seventh day in a far-off, other-worldly heaven quite remote from me. Advanced years have brought the realization that creation is here and now, and that the Creator is very much here and now, separating sea and dry land, sand and water, fairway grass and knee-high grass, and calling the results golf courses. That discovery has improved my golf only by improving my life and my attitudes toward the things of life. Hence, though this is not one of those books that promises to take ten strokes off your game, it is nonetheless a book that has helped me and might also help you.

It is ostensibly a book about golf but it is really a book about life and religion. The greatest need in a human life is the need for meaning, the need to feel bound and rooted, the need to be something more than a sliced drive blown further adrift by the wind. Religion is the human activity that binds men and women to their origin and their goal and roots them in ultimate meanings.

A book of prayers is easily recognizable as a religious activity. This book of prayers seeks to be that, but it seeks to be more. It seeks to be an acknowledgment that religion is about not only the great ultimate things in life, like birth and sex and death, but also about the many non-ultimate things, even that very non-ultimate and apparently meaningless activity called golf.

To some people golf is a sport; to others it is a business; to yet others it is a disease. In this book it is a paradigm for life and religion. Ordinary, commonplace golfing situations, well known to every weekend golfer, are here enlarged on the broader canvas of life and are rooted ultimately by religious meaning. I know of no other book that does this. It states very concretely what is frequently said very abstractly, namely, that the binding and the rooting achieved in life by religion extend well beyond those areas of life explicitly defined as religious. They extend even to golf. It will benefit readers by reflecting for them, and forcing them therefore to reflect on, the connectedness of golf, religion, and life. It has been my experience that, once this connectedness becomes clear, it is not difficult to realize that the same connectedness holds for everything else in life.

I wanted originally to describe this book as a book of spiritual theology. I was discouraged from doing so by my fifteen-year-old golf fanatic who persuaded me that no golfer would read a book of spiritual theology, since that is only for religious fanatics. I see now that he was wrong in his judgment and that I was wrong to listen to him. Spirituality is nothing more than the working out in our concrete lives of the religious beliefs we hold. A great many people have come to realize that, and to realize also that spirituality is not only for fanatics, saints, gurus, and holy women, but also for the simplest man and woman who believes in the God who loved us enough to create golf courses and us to walk and to play on them.

This book seeks to uncover the fact that, since God created golf courses, golf is one of those everyday human activities in which God is present and active and waiting to be discovered. That discovery has improved my golf, good or bad though it be, only by improving my attitude toward it. I can promise you only that it will do the same for you.

A Prayer at a Journey's Beginning

Lord God, like us, your Son set out on many journeys:
    from Bethlehem to Egypt,
    from Egypt to Nazareth,
    and up and down the dusty roads
    from there to Jerusalem.
I believe, therefore, that he will know the feel
    of setting out:
    the added adrenaline, the anxiety, the knotted stomach.
I describe myself, of course,
    as I stand on every First tee.
I know what troubles await on this golfing journey,
    for I have made it,
    and have found troubles in it,
    a thousand times before.
He knew too what awaited him
    in Egypt and in Jerusalem,
    yet he set his face into the desert wind
    to go there.
I confess that I find courage
    in the way he faced his journeys.
As I set out anew with my clubs on my shoulder,
    I borrow his prayer for journeys.
Let this cup of troubles pass from me.
But, then, not my will but yours be done.
Amen.

2

A Prayer of Thanks and Praise

Lord, God of all creation,
  we bless you
  for your grass and trees
  and sand and water,
  but mostly for your golf courses.
We praise you for the birdies
  you have made to fly,
  and beg of you more birdies
  that are made to drop.
If this request o'ersteps the bounds
  of your command to "ask and you will receive,"
  we shall be grateful still
  for plentiful pars.
Deliver us from all bogeys,
  double or simply single.
Amen.

3

A Prayer for Wisdom

Lord God, who fashioned men and women
    as symbolic animals,
    fashion us anew into women and men
    who can live as such.
Give us eyes to see
    that there is more to seeing
    than meets the eye;
    give us ears to hear far behind the ear drum.
When Jeremiah dashes a purchased pot
    to the ground,
    when Jesus proclaims at a sacred meal,
    "This is my body,"
    when lovers incarnate their love
    in words or roses or kisses,
    teach us to see through the dark surface
    of the symbols
    to the bright center where meanings hold.
In life as in golf,
    forgive us when we put ourselves, and you, in traps
    when we deny our nature and are unthinking.
Amen.

4

A Prayer for Courage

Lord God, Jesus your Christ made the journey
    all men and women make from birth to death.
He confronted the journey's troubles:
    a cold crib, a wicked king,
    a pusillanimous procurator
    whose gutlessness ended his journey.
We pray for what Pontius lacked:
    courage to face our troubles in life
    and on golf courses where we hide from life.
We seek this courage
    secure in the knowledge
    that we are in the hands of you, our Father,
    without whom not one sparrow or paltry putt falls.
We believe that you responded
    to Jesus' righteous courage
    by raising him to yourself at his journey's end.
We ask that you be with us
    and that you grant us courage,
    now to hit shots that lead to life,
    and at the end to face fearlessly endless life.
Amen.

A Prayer to Tread the Narrow Way

Lord God, I confess that your Christ is the Way
    that leads to truth and to life.
But I confess also
    that sometimes I find his Way
    narrower than tight fairways.
To the right of it are broad ways
    that lead to plastic places,
    filled with neon people and weekend commitments.
To the left of it are lakes that promise
    cool to the hot, and clean to the dusty, wayfarer.
But they deliver only death in the mud
    whence you brought us all to life.
Grant us reverence for the Golden Rule:
    straight down the narrow fairway,
    across the corner of the lake,
    a pitch, two putts for a bogey, one for a par.
It works for golfers;
    it should work also for pilgrims;
    but only with your help.
Do not withhold it, we pray you.
Amen.

6

A Prayer to Love Samaritans

Lord God, you taught us,
    "Love your neighbor as yourself."
I am happy that when you asked,
    "Who is my neighbor?"
    you did not reply, "Your golf partner."
For mine is so hard to love.
Unlike me, he always arrives late for our tee time.
Unlike me, he jabbers incessantly
    (especially when I am putting).
Unlike me, he manages never to buy a drink
    at the Nineteenth.
Thank you for asking us to love Samaritans,
    and not this miserable golfer.
What's that you say?
"Samaritan" means golf partner?
You're asking me to love this muttering miser
    whose hand sticks in his pocket
    when time comes to pay?
You really think that you could love him,
    and so could I?
Then, I beg of you, Lord, teach me
    to love Samaritans.
Amen.

A Prayer for Light

Lord God, who delivers golfers
    from fairway forests,
    lead us to see that,
    though you live in light ineffable,
    it is not only on golf courses
    that we live in darkness.
We beg you to shine your light
    through the dark windows that conceal you from us
    and from all who seek you in truth.
Reveal to us,
    as you revealed to your apostle Paul,
    that "now we see in a mirror dimly,
    but then face to face."
Confirm us in our search for you
    in the darkness.
Confirm others in their search for you
    through different windows.
But move us all to listen to you
    "No eye has seen, nor ear heard,
    nor the human heart conceived,
    what God has prepared
    (including the absolute sight of him)
    for those who love him."
Since our eyes do not see clearly
    in the darkness that hides you from us,
    grant us, we pray, at least ears
    to hear your word.
Amen.

8

A Prayer for Humility

Lord God, you once instructed Moses
    that you were God, not he.
I confess I have no problem with that instruction
    anywhere but on the golf course.
There, for some inexplicable reason,
    I expect to stand wrong,
    to hold the club wrong, and swing wrong,
    and yet, somehow, to hit a nifty Nicklausian shot.
I know it is quite unreasonable,
    for I have seen the great Nicklaus set up wrong
    and mail the ball to a neighboring patio,
    proving that he, like Moses, is not God.
I have been reminded regularly, of course,
    that I am not God,
    mostly by people who believe they are.
"Humility is truth," my golf partners tell me.
Therefore, when I get it all wrong,
    I should not act aggrieved
    toward the club or the ball
    or, still less, the partner,
    but should punish pride by confessing I am not God.
Since you know how difficult that is for me,
    I ask you not necessarily to make it easy for me,
    but to help me make it easy for myself.
Teach me this refrain:
    Moses is not God.
    Nicklaus is not God.
    I am not God.
Only God is God—thank God.
Amen.

9

A Prayer for Refreshment

Lord God, I've heard your invitation:
  "Come to me all who labor and are burdened,
  and I will give you rest."
Now, as I labor up heartbreak hill,
  weary and bag-burdened,
  it seems a good time
  to reflect on what you might have meant.
My body is tired,
  and looking forward to its refreshment:
  a Coke, perhaps a beer, and a hot dog.
I doubt, though, that is the refreshment
  you had in mind.
But more than my body is burdened.
After eight hellish holes,
  my spirit's strength is sapped.
It needs respite and steadfast support.
I believe this is what you offer.
You, your Son whom you sent among us,
  your Spirit whom you also sent
  that we might live your life,
  are refreshment to our oft-broken spirits.
Paul knew this long ago.
"Who will deliver me from the body of this death?
Thanks be to God through Jesus Christ our Lord."
Thanks be to God indeed. And Hosannah!
I accept your invitation,
and I come for rest.
Amen.

10

A Prayer for Renewal

Lord God, as I stand on this Tenth tee,
    I feel as though I have just responded
    to your invitation delivered through Jesus,
    "Come away to a desert place and rest awhile."
I reached the Ninth green
    drained and despondent.
But refreshment and reflection in the snack bar
    restored body and spirit
    and I am ready again for the fray.
Since this has happened many times before,
    I thought there must be a lasting lesson
    not only for my golf
    but also for my life.
    There are many times when,
    busy about many things,
    my spirit sags and I want to cry out with Jesus,
    "My God, my God, why have you forsaken me?"
I learn again today
    that I do not need angels to comfort me,
    but only to retreat from busy-ness
    to restfulness in you.
But you know well that busy-ness
    returns with forgetfulness.
I beg of you not to forget me,
    though I forget you.
Even if I cease to listen,
    do not cease to call me to come away.
Amen.

A Prayer in Selective Praise of Creation

Lord God, your holy people Israel
    was originally a desert people
    and then a sea people.
Sand was a powerful presence in its life.
As you will recall, you created me by the ocean
    and made sand a presence in my life.
I have used it to imagine an innumerable number,
    as you did when you promised Abraham
    you would make his descendants
    numerous as the sands of the sea.
I have used it, again like you,
    though with small success,
    to set bounds to the sea,
    a perpetual, impassable barrier.
In my life, Lord, sand has been
    more often a barrier to golf balls than to seas.
From St. Andrews to Hilton Head to Nebraska,
    sand-filled holes that would never trap seas
    have trapped my best-hit shots.
I confess I love your sand-creation on the beach,
    but I hate it on the golf course.
Move me, I pray you, to love you always,
    even on those occasions
    when I hate your creation,
    as I do now deep in this pot-belly bunker
    on Eleven.
Amen.

A Prayer of Thanks for Revelation

Lord God, I thank you for your revelation
    concerning borrows,
      those tantalizing turns on putting greens
      that poor putters like me can only dimly decipher.
The revelation was this:
If you created all things,
    then you created borrows.
If you created borrows,
      then you must know how to read them.
I ask you now to please read them for me.
I seek no advantage over those putters
    who do not speak to you.
I have no objection to your telling them too
      whether the borrow turns right or left
      and by how much.
For when I know how it turns,
    my putter will do the rest.
I do not know why I took so long to learn
      that if faith can move mountains,
      it can surely read borrows.
I fear I have missed many mysteries about you.
I fear I have concentrated so hard on putts
      that I have not heard your advice about borrows.
Forgive my deafness and my slowness to believe
      that you can read borrows
      as readily as you read the hearts of golfers.
Grant me to see both through your eyes.
Amen.

13

A Prayer for Golfers

Lord God, you first elected Israel
    as your special people,
    and then also the Christ-community called church.
We ask you now to choose golfers too as your people,
    and to bring us to a land of milk and honey,
    of beautiful birdies, plentiful pars,
    and very occasional bogies.
You know how we love this game you created.
You know how it schools us
    in faith and trust and steadfastness,
    and most of all in humility
    and, therefore, in passionate hope.
We believe that you are the creator
    who puts all things in their proper place.
We ask you to put our golf in its proper place,
    that is, after you.
We trust you will lead us,
    if not into the land of great golf,
    then into the land of lasting life with you.
Have compassion on us in our tribulations,
    though we inflict them,
    and high blood pressure, on ourselves.
We hope that in our present land
    of blighted bogies and lonesome pars
    we can remember your promise
    of unimaginable everlasting life.
We trust you not to burden us
    with yet one more disappointment.
Amen.

14

A Prayer for Perseverance

Lord God, I have understood nowhere better
    than on golf-courses the meaning of Jesus' saying:
    "No one who puts his hand to the plow and looks back
    is fit for the Kingdom of God."
On the back nines of golf courses I come to know
    the context of the saying in my life.
I stand on First tees with such unconcern.
Hope obliterates memory
    and I tell myself mendaciously
    that I will play better this time.
It is always about Fourteen that I know I have lied
    and disillusionment sets in, for it is no better.
Once more I have garnered
    more double bogies than single pars.
To complete the round is drudgery,
    much like the many days
    when I find it impossible to live the life I should.
I brought to baptism the same unconcern
    I brought to the First tee.
Ignorant of the trials ahead,
    Christ-life seemed so simple.
Now I know, and I am tempted to drop my clubs and my plow
    and to seek more peaceful, less problematic, pastures.
But golf has taught me one thing: to finish well.
Small successes obliterate large failures
    and return me to hope.
I trust you, Lord, to look upon my small successes
    as passes to your Kingdom.
Do not expect, though, neatly furrowed fields of success.
Amen.

15

A Prayer for Life

Lord God, you bring life from water,
    pouring it on clay until it is the fertile mud
    from which you fashion men and women, *adam*.
You deliver also death from water,
    in floods great and small.
We acknowledge you as the Lord of life
    and the Lord of death,
    as the creator who conquers water
    and who puts it in its proper place.
Deliver us, we pray you,
    from the water and the mud
    that deal deserved death to unthinking golfers.
If this request is too importunate for a busy God,
    deliver us, then, simply from death.
Daughters and sons of *adam*,
    we do not ask that we not die.
We ask, rather,
    that whenever and wherever and however we die,
    we die, like Jesus, in your hands,
    so that, like Jesus,
    we may be raised to lasting life with you
    and exult.
"Hosannah! At last an eagle. Alleluia."
Amen.

16

A Prayer for Fruitfulness

Lord God, sower who sows good seed,
    I believe you have sowed your seed in me.
But I am Zacchaeus,
    ground that has been trodden hard.
I fear for your life-laden seed.
I am such rocky ground;
    it might lose its life entering me;
I am such arid ground;
    Its life might dry up in me;
I am such cold ground;
    its life might freeze in me;
I am such thorn-covered ground;
    even if it takes root in me,
    its life might yet be choked.
Yet I feel a stirring in me to welcome your seed,
    a silent surge that encourages me to hope
    that you will clear and warm and water this ground
    as you warm and water and nourish
    your golf courses in spring.
Do not, I pray you,
    leave me barren as fairway trees in winter,
    but ready me for fertile summer,
    when I might shoot
    not only Ballesteros-birdies and Palmer-pars,
    but also Jesus-justice that bears good fruit.
Amen.

A Prayer for Forgiveness

Lord God, you taught us to pray,
    "Forgive us our trespasses,
    for we have forgiven those
    who trespass against us."
I need today to forgive myself,
    for I have trespassed tremendously against myself.
On One, I left a four wood short.
On Seven, I hooked a drive out of bounds.
On Thirteen, I lofted an easy seven iron into the lake.
You, who sees the golfer's hidden heart,
    know that the four wood is enough
    for two hundred yards;
    that my position at address
    should have caused the ball to fade;
    that I have hit a thousand seven-irons
    across that little lake.
Paul had such days in mind, I believe,
    when he screamed,
    "I do not do what I want,
    but I do the very thing I hate."
I take comfort in that today
    as I trudge up Seventeen.
I beg you to notice that I have forgiven myself,
    so that you can be moved
    to forgive me for the several times
    I called out your name—
    in vain.
Amen.

A Prayer at a Journey's End

Lord God, you created journeys
    and the men and women who make them.
Some journeys you made as short as par threes.
They challenge briefly
    but soon we pass them by.
Some journeys you made par fives,
    demanding dedicated self-sacrifice for a lifetime.
It is on these life-long journeys
    that we have trouble and are tempted to turn back.
Among these journeys you have created a foursome:
    Religion, Sex, Death, and Golf,
    which we find terrible.
We pray you, then,
    to bless us bountifully along these ways,
    or we shall look constantly back
    to become Lot's-wife pillars.
Grant us, we pray you,
    to finish Eighteens with a flourish, so that we might learn
to finish well
    all the fearsome four.
If we only could,
    we would laughingly praise you forever.
Amen.

A Prayer for Election

Lord God, you led Israel from Egypt
    into a lustrous land.
You led Jesus from death
    into lasting life with you.
Lead us, we pray you,
    through lakes and traps and trees
    into a land flowing
    with plentiful pars and beautiful birdies.
You established the sacred meals, seder and eucharist,
    to be the vehicles for remembering
    the elections of Israel and of Jesus and his people.
We established the Ninteenth Hole
    as our memorial meal.
When Israelites gather for seder
    and when Christians gather for eucharist,
    their ancient tears are long-dried
    by your wonderful works.
When we golfers gather at the Nineteenth,
    our tears flow still
    for pains too recent to forget.
We ask you to elect golfers too as your people
    and to dry our tears,
    so that we can say at our sacred meal,
    as Israelites and Christians say at theirs,
    you are our God who saves us always.
Amen.